WHAT WAS LIFE LIKE ON THE FRONTIER?

US History Books for Kids
Children's American History

Speedy Publishing LLC

40 E. Main St. #1156

Newark, DE 19711

www.speedypublishing.com

Copyright 2017

Life on the frontier was full of hard work and difficulties. Once the farmer had cleared the land, planted the crops, and built a cabin and barn, there was still a lot of work that had to be done every day. The entire family had to help out in order to survive. Every day, these settlers would wake up at sunrise and work until sunset. In this book, we will be learning about exactly what life was like on the frontier.

WHERE DO WE BEGIN?

The farmers had to start by building a cabin and a barn. The barn was needed to keep the animals safe from the wolves and other predators, as well as a place to store grain and farm tools. The cabin and barn were typically made from logs in a way that didn't require nails.

It was a lot of work for the farmer to plant seed on the big farm. He would first have to plow the field using a large plow that was pulled by oxen or by a horse. He would next scatter the seeds about the fields, and then finally would use the horse to cover the seeds with dirt.

WOMEN ON THE FRONTIER

The women worked at their own jobs. They would also often help the farmer during harvesting and planting times in the fields. Some of their other tasks included:

They would make soap from water, lye, and ashes obtained from the fireplace

Spinning wool to make yarn, or flax to make thread

Tend to the garden so their family would have several types of vegetables

Repairing and sewing the clothes for their family

New York City, 1890

WHAT DID THE CHILDREN DO?

The children were put to work as soon as they were able to help, even as young as four or five years of age. They would get water from a stream nearby, keep an eye on the fire to make sure it did not go out, keep the cows and the chickens from eating their crops, they would milk the cows in the morning, and then churn it into butter.

As they grew older, the children would take on tasks that were more difficult. Older boys would often chop wood or work the farm. The older daughters would help take care of their younger brothers and sisters.

Museum of American Frontier Culture

WHAT WAS SCHOOL LIKE ON THE FRONTIER?

Some of the children of the frontier would attend a local schoolhouse that was one room. They typically had one teacher that taught all grades and they would learn the basics including writing, reading, spellings, history, and math. They would use slates instead of paper for writing. Slates were similar to small chalkboards that they held in their hands.

They would typically attend school during the summer and the winter, but would stay home during the planting and harvesting seasons to help on the farm.

American Farm, Museum of American Frontier Culture

Museum of American Frontier Culture

WHAT DID THEY DO FOR FUN ON THE FRONTIER?

While they mostly worked, occasionally they would get together for fun at a picnic or a dance. They would sometimes work together on a big job, perhaps building a barn, and once it was completed, they would hold a dance in the barn. For music, they played accordions and fiddles.

The kids would enjoy playing outdoor games and swimming. The did not have many toys bought from a store, so they would have to create their own. The young girls would practice their sewing skills and make themselves dolls to play with.

HOW DID WEATHER AFFECT LIFE ON THE FRONTIER?

The pioneers depended heavily on the weather. A drought might kill their crops, wiping out all the work they had done for the year. Even worse, wildfires could possibly destroy everything they had, including the crops, house, and barn. They also had to fear insects consuming their crops as well as tornadoes that could destroy their home. It was not an easy, comfortable life.

THE LOG CABIN HOMES

Once the pioneers arrived at their new land, they needed to build a home for their family to live in. If there were plenty of trees around, they would construct a log cabin.

Log Cabin

Few resources were needed to build a log cabin, only the trees and either a saw or an axe. Metal nails or spikes were not needed to hold the logs together and the cabins went up fairly quickly. They were typically a one room building for the whole family to live in. When the farm was up and running, the pioneers would often build a bigger home or add on to the log cabin they had built earlier.

CLEARING THE LAND

The settlers first had to clear land to build the house on. They would make sure there was land around the home to plant their garden, build their barn, and keep animals, such as chickens. They would sometimes have to cut down trees and remove the stumps when clearing the land. These trees would then be used for building the log cabin.

BUILDING THE WALLS

The four walls would be built using one log at a time. At each end, hey would cut notches into the logs so the logs would snugly fit each other. If just one person was building the cabin, it would typically be 6 or 7 feet tall, since he could lift the log only so high. The walls could be a little bit taller if he had help.

The sides of the cabin typically were between 12 and 16 feet long. When the roof and the walls were completed, they would seal the cracks with clay or mud. This was referred to as "chinking" or "daubing" the walls.

Log Cabin Interior

Fireplace

THE FINISHING TOUCHES

At one end of the cabin, they would build a stone fireplace to keep them warm and to use for cooking. Typically, there would be one or two windows for letting the light in, but they seldom had glass available to them. They would mostly use greased paper for covering the windows. The floors typically were packed earth, but occasionally they would use split logs for the floor.

WHAT DID THE SETTLERS USE FOR FURNITURE?

They didn't have much furniture, particularly when they would first move in; they might have a bed, a table, and one or two chairs. They would often have a chest that they brought along from their homeland, which may have included decorations such as candlesticks or a rug that they used to make the cabin feel like their home.

Cowboys

WHO WERE THE COWBOYS?

They played a key role in settling the west. Ranching was huge, and the cowboys assisted with running these ranches. They would herd cattle, repair buildings and fences, and take care of the horses.

WHAT IS A CATTLE DRIVE?

The cowboys worked a lot on the cattle drives. This is when they would move a big herd of cattle from the ranch to the marketplace to be sold. Several of the original cattle drives went from Texas to Kansas.

Cattle Drive

The cowboys would start early "guiding" the herd to the next point where they would stop for the night. The senior cowboys got to ride at the front, and the junior riders had to be in the back because of the dust resulting from the herd.

There would typically be about a dozen riders for a herd of approximately 3000 cattle. Also included would be a wrangler, a camp cook, and a trail boss. Usually, the wrangler would be a junior cowboy whose job it was to keep track of any extra horses.

Cattle Round Up

THE ROUNDUP

Every spring and fall, the cowboys would work the "roundup", which was the process of the cowboys bringing in the cattle from an open range. Most of the year, the cattle roamed freely, but at some point, they had to bring them in.

All cattle had a "brand" which was a marking burned into them so they could tell what cattle belong to the ranch they were working.

HORSE AND SADDLE

A cowboy's horse and his saddle were his most important possession. The saddles typically were custom made and, next to their horse, probably the cowboy's most valuable item. Since their horses were so important to them, theft of a horse was considered a hanging offense!

CLOTHING

Cowboys wore 10-gallon hats in order to protect them from the rain and the sun. The boots had pointed toes which helped slipping in and out of stirrup when riding their horse. This was also important so they would not be dragged by the horse if they fell off of it.

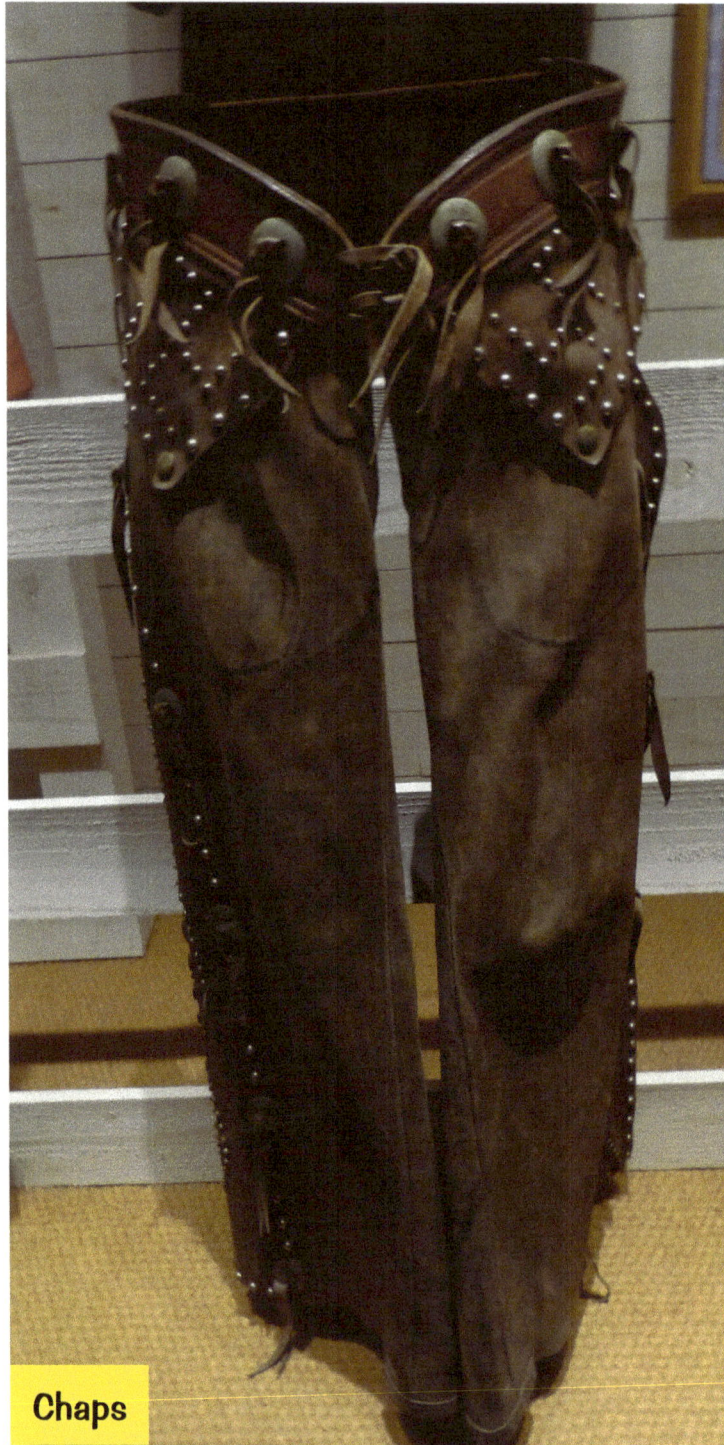

Chaps

Wearing chaps on their legs helped to protect them from cacti and sharp bushes that they might rub against while riding the horse. They would also wear a bandana over most of their face to keep protect them from the dust the cattle would create.

THE COWBOY CODE

Cowboys in the Old West had an unwritten code that they lived by that included rules such as always say "howdy", be courteous, never ride another man's horse unless you have permission, don't wave at someone on a horse (nod instead), never wear someone else's hat, and always assist someone that needs help.

Rodeo

RODEO

A Rodeo is a competition that has events based on the cowboy's daily jobs such as steer wrestling, calf roping, bareback bronco riding, barrel racing, and bull riding.

Life on the frontier was definitely a lot of hard work. However, it is because of those hard workers that we are able to enjoy life as we know it. If you would like to learn more about life on the frontier, you can visit your local library, research the internet, and ask questions of your teachers, family and friends.

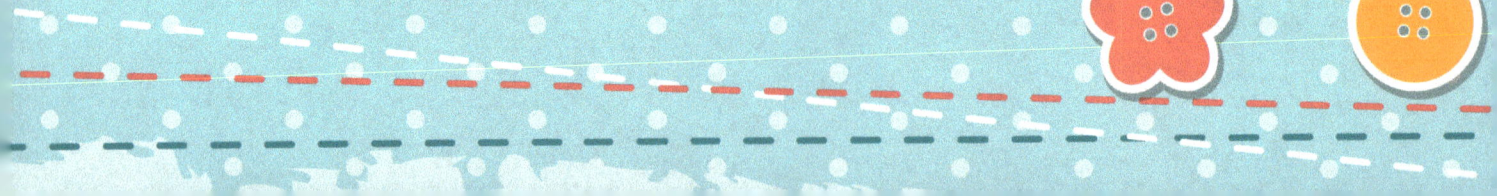

Visit

BABY PROFESSOR
EDUCATION KIDS

www.BabyProfessorBooks.com

to download Free Baby Professor eBooks
and view our catalog of new and exciting
Children's Books

Milton Keynes UK
Ingram Content Group UK Ltd.
UKHW050931310824
447642UK00002B/189

9 798869 414410